GW00808814

The Ultimate Guide to Raising Healthy Koi

How to Keep Your Koi Fish
Happy and Healthy, Without
Spending a Fortune

By
Arthur Flynn

Table of Contents

Introduction:
A Little History

Welcome! I'm glad you have an interest in koi and am thrilled you found this book. If you've been thinking about raising koi, but procrastinating because you thought they were too difficult to take care of, think again.

Maybe you hesitated because you really didn't know where to start. Or maybe you've never kept fish before and thought you should begin with "starter" fish.

I'm here to tell you right now that if it's koi you want in your aquarium or pond, then it's koi you should have. Don't let anyone to talk you out of it.

These amazing fish are among the most beautiful alive. They provide hours of entertainment and joy, and create an abundance of naturally calming emotions. They're not just for show; you can use them to help rest your tired, tangled nerves after a hard day at work.

You may be interested to know that you're not alone in your admiration of these amazingly colorful fish. The koi -- or as they say in Japan *nishikigoi* (meaning "colored koi") -- are the most popular freshwater fish for pond owners.

And with good reason. Just gaze at their grace, beauty, and colors, even for a short time. You'll soon discover that it's difficult *not* to fall in love with this one-of-a-kind fish.

Would you believe that a creature this beautiful and graceful is also easy to care for? It's true! Once you see how extremely easy these fish are to call your own, you'll be wondering why you didn't start this hobby sooner.

And you'll love the fact that koi live a relatively long life (as fish lives go).

Some koi keepers take pride in the fact that they are continuing a tradition that began thousands of years ago.

In Japan, koi have historically been symbols of strength and masculinity. They are widely known in that country as "warrior's fish." (It doesn't get much more masculine than that!)

The Japanese also see these fish as symbols of good luck and prosperity. So admired are these fish, that streamers in the shape of koi can be seen everywhere in the country each year in May. The streamers celebrate the Boy's Day Festival and the koi pictured on them represent parents' most sincere hope that their sons demonstrate courage and strength.

You'll be amazed at the seemingly unlimited variety of colors and patterns that koi exhibit (and we'll talk about this in the next chapter). Many people think these variations indicate different species of fish, but they don't. There is just one koi, or *Cyprinius carpio*, and its exciting variations are simply for our pleasure.

Did you notice that last half of the scientific name of the fish? *Carpio*. If you think that koi might be members of the carp family, you're absolutely right.

It's no accident that there are so many different koi to choose from today. The variety is the result of careful and thoughtful selective breeding conducted over several hundreds of years.

How Old Are Koi?

Koi are a rare kind of fish. They're almost considered mythological creatures in Japan.

10

The facts and myths about these fish have been intertwined and embellished throughout the years. It's difficult for even the best authorities on the subject to tell where history stops and fable begins.

And it's odd to see such a tradition grow around fish.

Ask three separate authorities on the precise historical point at which the varied color of koi were first observed, and you'll get three distinctly different answers. And for heaven's sake, don't even bother to ask them who first recorded the existence of koi -- a fistfight is liable to break out.

You are beginning to see the larger picture. Much of the history of the koi -- especially the ancient history -- is shrouded in a vague fog, clouded by time, colored by folktales, and embellished by stories handed down from one generation to the next.

It's believed by at least some of the most respected authorities that the fish are native to Persia. They were taken from their home country by various visitors stunned and infatuated by their beauty. That is how they began their journey around the world.

From Persia, their travels can be directly traced to China and Japan.

It's believed that these beautiful fish originally began as common-looking fish. How common, you wonder? According to some experts, koi were originally a drab gray. They foraged in streams, sifting the bottom of the stream bed for food.

Rugged and hardy, koi were an important source of food for many people. But beautiful, they were not!

Colorful Koi

References to koi with color appear in a Chinese book as far back as the Western Chin Dynasty. For those of you who aren't up on the dates of the royal houses of China (and few of us are!), that dynasty lasted from 265 to 316 AD. (This is even before Constantine declared Christianity the religion of the Byzantine Empire!)

This particular ancient book discusses carp of wide color variations, including black, blue, white, and red. The question remains: how exactly did these fish develop these colors? Did people interfere with nature via deliberate breeding techniques?

Or did these fish just spontaneously mutate into different colors? These questions will probably never be answered to anyone's satisfaction.

The one thing that seems clear is that the Japanese took a proactive view of selective breeding. They became the undisputed leaders in breeding koi -- and still are today.

Koi: The Modern Story

And that brings us to a portion of koi history called the modern period. Breeding these fish began in earnest in the 17th century, in an area of Japan called Niigata Prefecture. It's a region renown for its rice production.

The farmers in this region took notice of these dismally gray carp because, on occasion, the fish would produce offspring with a different color or body pattern. After diligent study, the farmers were able to establish several distinct varieties of colorful koi.

Fast forward two hundred years. Now it's the 19th century, and there's an explosion of koi farmers breeding these fish. New color varieties are being developed in the region.

If you're at all familiar with koi, then you

may recognize the variety *kohaku*,
developed during this time period. This once
drab fish -- traditionally used only as food --
became a wildly popular ornamental fish.
In fact, it was fast becoming the era's
"fashion statement." Eventually this koi
became known as the "fish of the nobility."

But at that point in history, koi didn't have
the international notoriety they enjoy today.
Even at the beginning of the 20th century,
their fame and the admiration were
confined to the Niigata region of Japan.

But that soon changed. In 1914, an
exposition was held in Tokyo. Some of the
most beautiful koi of the Niigata region
were transported and shown at the expo.

Do I have to tell you the rest of the story?
I'm sure you're well ahead of me by now.
The koi's appearance in Tokyo marked the
first time this colorful fish had ever been
seen by people outside of the village region.

People went "koi crazy." Some of the best
specimens were presented to Crown Prince
Hirohito. It wasn't long before the entire
country was talking about koi. Soon, their
popularity spread to other areas of the
world.

As the fish's popularity grew, the major pedigree lines became established. This provided for the development of even more varieties. During the twentieth century, the varieties of koi exploded.

The most skilled of the breeders use a combination of traditional techniques and modern genetics, bearing in mind the historical line of the fish. Every year, more varieties are developed and presented to the public.

If you happen to be a Japanese breeder of certain pedigree lines, your fish could be especially prized. Many of these fish command large amounts of money when sold today. It's common for some breed specimens to sell for upwards of $15,000 to $20,000.

It wasn't until the 1950s, though, that koi became popular in the West. And it really wasn't until the 1980s that koi really sparked the imagination of America. That era experienced a rise in the interest of ornamental garden ponds, and with it, a natural interest in koi.

And that brings us to today. More people than ever before are discovering the beauty of these irresistible fish. And you, obviously, are one of them.

How to Use This Book Wisely

First, take your time (go ahead and get a
cup of coffee or tea if you'd like!) and read
through the entire book. Get a feel for the
koi -- what they look like, their likes, their
dislikes. Even get a good idea of what type
of diseases they may be prone to, too.

You'll find all of that in this guide, and
more. After you read through these
chapters once, you may want to go back
over one or two of them again. This is
especially true if you're planning on buying
koi.

Before you run out to adopt your fish, re-
read the appropriate chapters. Double-
check what you need to buy *before* you
bring your friends home. It would be
terrible to discover you're missing a key koi
ingredient while the poor fish wait in plastic
bags pondering their fate.

The overall purpose of the book is not only
to help you decide whether koi would be a
good hobby for you, but also to help you
bring them into your life and care for them
in as stress-free a way as possible.

That's why there's a chapter spent on describing koi, as well as one spent on outlining the diseases they may contract. Heck, I've even included a chapter on what's required to build your own koi pond should you be thinking in that direction.

What I've shared here in this book is basically my love of this glorious fish and my knowledge of how to adopt them, love them, and keep them healthy and happy for a long time.

Chapter 1:
On Being Koi

It does resemble a goldfish, doesn't it? And that's not simply a coincidence. Scientifically, the koi is a member of a family whose name is **Cyprinidae.** While that name probably means nothing to you, zoologists who read this are nodding their heads in total agreement.

Without a doubt, koi belong to same large family as goldfish, minnows, and as we mentioned earlier, carp.

In fact, if you really want to suck the romance out of your fascination with koi, you may want to look at them as merely domesticated carp. But never a fish, you say, domesticated so well! Indeed, you're right.

Koi have been selectively bred for their colors and color patterns. No surprise here. They're freshwater, bottom-dwelling fish, and you'll find these gorgeous legendary creatures primarily in temperament climates. Surprisingly, though, koi can live in a wide range of weather conditions.

Take a good look at the rounded body of the koi. It's called a "fusiform" shape. This means the thickest portion of the animal is in its middle, and it slowly tapers towards both ends.

Koi are excellent at quickly darting away from their predators. Hmm? Would you say then that koi are, well...*coy*?

Wild carp, the original ancestors of these beautiful koi, are found worldwide. They feed on plants, worms, and insects...to name just a few of their favorite foods. Carp can reach a length of more than three feet, and they can weigh more than 25 pounds.

Koi can live surprisingly long lives. Some have been known to reach the age of 40 and older. If you're around koi keepers long enough, you're bound to hear about certain members of the species living to be 200 years. (Take those reports with a grain of salt; you've probably ventured into the realm of myth at that point.)

Here's Looking At You, Koi!

Koi are considered a "bony" fish. They have features and characteristics shared by many bony fish, but also possess certain physical traits unique to their specific species.

The fins found in the mid-body of the koi are called **medial fins.** All of these are single. The **dorsal** -- one of the medial fins -- is large and extends back. The fish lowers this fin when it's swimming fast to help keep it upright in the water.

The **tail fin** -- also called a **caudal** -- is forked. It is used to help propel the fish forward. And on its ventral surface ("ventral" is just a more sophisticated name for "bottom"!) a lone **anal fin** is in place to stabilize the fish's swimming.

You'll also notice that the **lateral fins** are all paired. Lateral fins are those found on either side of the koi. The **pelvic fins**, for example, can be found just in front of the anal fin. This pair helps the fish to move up and down.

If you look closely, you'll discover yet another set of fins just behind the fish's gills. These are called the **pectoral fins.** The fish uses them to stop and to help make turns.

Is That Koi Smiling At Me?

The mouth of the koi is located just about where you'd expect it to be for a bottom dweller, at the end of the snout. It lies slightly below the midline of the animal. Positioned here, it allows the koi to feed entirely -- and efficiently -- on the bottom of a pond or stream.

Look at those **barbuls**. Those are the whisker-like tactile organs similar to the type you find on catfish. These richly endowed receptors detect food that may be hidden in sand or mud. In this way, koi don't need to actually *see* where their food is hidden. They can easily "touch" the location of their food. Pretty remarkable!

If you travel just a little bit farther up from the barbuls, located almost right between the eyes, you'll find a pair of nostrils. And these, not surprisingly, are used to sniff out odors.

Ears To The Koi

Kids love to ask certain puzzling questions. One of them always seems to be "Do fish have ears?" Usually this leaves adult puzzling and in turn asking the same thing.

Well in the case of koi, they really do have ears. Can't see them? I'm not surprised.

They're not external ears. But they do have organs of hearing.

The koi possesses an internal ear. That may seem like a paradox for humans with their need for an external ear, but this arrangement suits the koi quite well.

Their internal ear actually "listens" in conjunction with their **swim bladder.** Sound waves cause the bladder to vibrate, and this vibration is then passed on to the *otoliths* of the inner ear. This stimulates the auditory nerves, which then signal the brain of the "sound."

As with other vertebrates (animals who have a backbone), the inner ear and, in this case the otoliths, also play a crucial role in maintaining equilibrium and balance.

What The Heck Are These?

If you examine your koi very closely, you'll notice a series of very small pores along its sides. Called lateral lines, these pores run midline from its head to its tail.

Believe it or not, these are another of your fishy friend's organs of "hearing." They detect low-frequency vibrations in the water, most notably those that might come from predators.

The Eyes Have It

The eyes of your koi are located just behind his nostrils. If you examine your fish closely (Is it getting tired of you staring at it yet?), one of the first things you'll see is that the fish lacks true eyelids. The covering over its eye is really a layer of transparent skin.

The lenses of its eyes are spherical and rigid. A koi focuses by moving the lens either forward of back within the eye itself.

What's a fish without gills? (And don't answer "Dead"!) The fish's gills allow a fish to breathe underwater. In the koi, you'll find them behind the eyes in something called the "branchial chambers."

Covered by a flap of skin and bone known as the *operculum*, each set of gills uses this flap to move water across the feathery organs. The gills contain tissue that possess rich networks of capillary -- tiny blood vessels -- designed especially for the purpose of gas exchange.

Dissolved oxygen is taken from the water and carbon dioxide and ammonia are then released.

And like most fish, koi are endowed with scales. The body of this fish is covered with a host of tiny scales. However, you can find some members of the species where the opposite is true. They're covered in a small number of larger scales. And don't be surprised if you encounter an occasional koi with no scales at all. Yes, a few of them really do exist.

If you were to look at a scale under a microscope, the first feature you would notice would be a series of concentric rings. Believe it or not, these rings can help scientists determine the age of the fish -- at least it provides them with a rough approximation.

You're probably thinking about tree trunks. Each ring on a tree represents a year of growth. (At least, that's what I was thinking when I first heard about this!)

But it doesn't work that way with koi. Each ring represents a period of growth, but these rings may not be directly related with any set amount of years. Scale-ring analysis, as it's called, can't be used to determine an absolute age for a fish.

Very often, a koi's scales overlap and actually project out of the skin at an angle. They're also covered with a layer of mucus. This reduces friction as the fish swims. Scales also provide protection from infections -- both bacterial and viral -- because the mucus covering contains antibodies.

What Gives Koi
Their Brilliant Colors?

Why genetic breeding, of course! But beyond that, physiologically, the colors of the koi are really a function of the pigments within the fish's skin. The type and distribution of these pigments determine the fish's color and patterning.

Specific cells actually contain very small sacs of pigment, which scientists refer to as *chromatophores*. These sacs are capable of holding more than one type of pigment, including one called *melanin* -- or black -- and others called *carotenoids*. It's the latter pigments which provide the brilliant variation in color.

Koi also have cells called *indocytes* that contain something called *guanine crystals*. These crystals give the fish's skin a shimmery gold and silver metallic appearance.

If you had the chance to view these cells through a powerful microscope, you would immediately notice that the chromatophore cells appear to have highly branched processes, which are ultimately connected to their nerve fibers.

This is the key to their ability to change color. If a koi is stressed because of illness or the poor quality of water, it may change to a lighter or a darker shade. All that's required for this feat is the movement of the pigment granules inside the cells.

If the pigment shifts to the center of the cell, the fish turns a lighter color. If the fish turns a darker color, then you know the pigment has moved to the outer areas of the cell.

What's Inside That Fish, Anyway?

Koi contain internal organs that are very common among all "bony" fish. These include digestive, excretory, circulatory, and reproductive systems.

The digestive system of this breed is marked by a long intestinal tract, but is void of any true stomach. The length of the tract, interestingly enough, correlates remarkably with the koi's vegetarian diet. Carnivores, or meat eaters, whether on land or underwater, normally have short intestines by comparison.

The long intestines allow for food to be ground as it passes through the pharyngeal teeth in the back of the throat. From there it goes to the esophagus and then to the gut. There, it's digested with the aid of enzymes and other secretions, some of which are provided by the koi's large liver.

The excretory system deals with the waste products of the digestive system. The products are released through the anus, which is near the anal fin. The gills also serve a function in this area. They act as excretory organs, releasing both ammonia and carbon dioxide.

As with other freshwater fish, koi have a problem when it comes to eliminating the excess water constantly entering their bloodstream. Water enters through the gills and other various body surfaces. This function gets the help of a kidney which is positioned close to the vertebrae. In addition to any extra water, the kidney also filters liquid wastes eliminated through the anus.

Koi Have Heart:
The Two-Chambered Kind

Right behind the gills, you'll find the koi's heart. A two-chambered organ, it's enclosed in what's called a *pericardial sac*. The heart pumps blood through the arteries which -- like ours -- are found throughout the entire body. The arteries subdivide until the capillaries are so tiny they're microscopic.

The exchanges between the tissue and the blood occur through these tiny capillaries, which eventually reunite to form larger veins. And the veins then carry the blood back to the heart. The gills allow deoxygenated blood from the periphery to mix with the re-oxygenated blood.

The two-chambered heart of the koi isn't as efficient as our four-chambered one. And because of this, the oxygen content of the fish's blood is more diluted. The end result is that the metabolism of fish is slower than that of mammals.

A Swim Bladder?

Yes, a swim bladder. The function of this

organ, which is probably new to you, is to control the buoyancy of the fish. In effect it controls the depth to which the fish can swim. Pretty cool!

Located near the backbone, this organ is large and filled with air. As I mentioned early, it is part of the sound receptor for the fish -- or "inner ear."

This bladder is prone to problems. And as you might expect, these problems could eventually lead to trouble with maintaining buoyancy. Usually, this is caused by some bacterial infection.

Physically, it's no surprise: all koi are created...well, if not *equal*, then at least *similar*. The similarities are the adhesive that hold them together as a species. The scientific community assesses what common traits the fish have, then classifies them accordingly.

But what makes this species so mesmerizing are the glorious differences in colors, patterns, and general appearance. If you've never seriously investigated the myriad categories of koi available for your pond, then hang on as you read the next chapter. It'll make your head spin -- *guaranteed!*

Chapter 2:
Here a Koi, There a Koi:
Which Koi's For You?

Ll of them are absolutely gorgeous, aren't they? So now that you've decided you want to be a koi keeper, how do you decide which variety to choose?

It helps if you acquire a passing familiarity with the varieties of koi available to you before you rush to the store or a breeder and make your final choice.

As you might imagine, there are different ways of labeling ornamental carp. Fish can be described and classified very differently, depending on where you live or what koi group you're involved with.

In addition to the presentation in this book, many hobbyists classify koi through a historical approach. The breakdowns involve the first varieties to appear, who was involved in the breeding process, and lineages.

And that's all well and good, and you may be enthusiastic enough to discover all that information one day. More power to you. But for the moment, the best method of classifying koi is through a physical description.

Here are just a few of the varieties you're likely to encounter by the time you're ready to call a koi your own.

Kohaku have a white body with red markings. Sometimes the markings appear to have a more orange tint than red. But whether they're red or orange, they're still known as kohaku.

If you encounter a koi that is predominately red (or *Hi* as is the strict Koi description for red) with some black markings, this fish is called the **Taisho Sanke** or sometimes known as the **Taisho Sanshoku**. When speaking about koi, the black markings are called *Sumi*.

Within this wide category, if you dare scratch the surface, you'll find even more designations of koi. For example, there exists a color-pattern combination known as the **Straight Hi.** The red coloring on these particular fish is best described as interconnecting "meandering islands" of red.

You may also find fish with red markings in which the red resembles a lightning bolt. And no, they aren't known as the "Harry

Potter" koi, but that was a good guess. Instead, they are called **Inazuma** and the red here is also interconnected.

If you see a Kohaku type of koi with what many call a "two-step pattern," then you've found a **Nidan**. *Ni*, by the way, means "two" in Japanese. This fish has two completely distinct "islands of red" on its body.

The **Sandan** has what is commonly called a "three-step" pattern. And yes, you're absolutely right. *San* means "three" in Japanese. And this koi is graced with three independent "islands" of red on his body.

Now, it's your turn to identify a koi. Let's say it has four islands of red, and they're not connected. *Yon* is the Japanese word for "four." If you guessed the fish is called **Yondan**, you're right! It's not so difficult to understand once you know the equation.

Some hobbyists will additionally sub-categorize these fish by identifying the markings on their head. One sub-category is called the **Kuchibeni.** This one is cute, indeed. The red markings around its mouth make it look as if it's wearing lipstick!

Another sub-category is **Menkaburi.** This

type of fish is often said to have "a hood on its head." The marking starts from behind and below the eyes and often extends to the mouth.

If you hear koi keepers describe a fish with a red crown on its head, then you know they're talking about the **Maruten**, a type of Kahoku that not only has red on its head, but carries a little more red on its body as well.

The **Showa Sanke**, sometimes called the **Show Sanshoku**, is a black-bodied koi with red and white markings. At first glance, you may confuse it with the **Taisho Sanke**. But the Showa has more black, including on the head in the margins of the pectoral and tail fins.

The next koi has a marking called "Red Sun" on its head, and that's really the only red marking it has. It's called a **Tancho.** The ideal example of this koi is found if the red doesn't bleed to other areas, is circular, and is centered on it head precisely. Good luck with that!

Bekko:
The Turtle Koi

Some koi hobbyists prefer the fish called

Bekko. Its solid body has black markings. Often confused with another variety called **utsuri**, the Bekko only have markings on their backs. One koi keeper I know calls them "turtles" because of this. (Turtles, if you haven't noticed, only have markings on their backs.)

The **Utsurimono**, although similar to Bekka as we have already noticed, is a black-bodied koi with markings of only a single color.

The koi called **Koroma** is similar to the Kohaku, but with additional colors of blue, black, and purple blended into the red. (The Koroma was cross-bred with the Asagi to produce this result.)

You may also find a type of koi called **Gin Rin.** This refers to the fish's scaling. It's not only a pearl-silver coloring, but it's reflective as well. Talk about stunning!

Related, but much harder to find, is the **Kin Rin.** In this variety, of koi the scales are a reflective pearl-gold coloring. If you can find one of these, you are one lucky koi keeper!

Sky Color Koi

34

Asagi refers to "sky color" and when it appears on a koi, it refers to a fish with a blue-gray body. Occasionally, this variety also possesses a red marking about midway onto its head and body.

The **Shusu** have large scales that are only found along the midline of the back or on its sides. In some instances, these scales are found in both areas. They may be mistaken for Asagi because their bodies are the same beautiful blue-gray.

The **Kawarimono** have sometimes been referred to as the "leftovers." But leftovers have never looked so striking! These koi are not metallic and they just don't seem to fit in any other category.

For lack of any other grouping, the following fish are usually found grouped together. This is especially true in fish shows.

The group known as **Hikarimuji** are not only single-colored, but they're metallic as well.

And they aren't to be confused with the similarly-named **Hikarimoyo**. This category describes a koi with two or more colors. Excluded from this is the **Hikari Utsuri.** The Hikari utsuri includes all of the metallic Show varieties.

There's another group called **Doitsu.** These fish are mirror-scaled koi. They have enlarged rows of scales along the midline of the back or on the sides of their bodies.

The name interestingly comes from the Japanese for "Deutsch" after the German-scaled carp. This fish initially was bred so it could be scaled easily for cooking purposes. Varieties of the Koitsu include the **Kohaku**, **Sanke**, and **Showa.**

Butterfly Koi

Another grouping is referred to as the **butterfly koi.** The name butterfly refers to the long fins this fish has in the front of its body.

How To
Purchase Koi

You're about to run out the door to adopt your new koi. Suddenly, coat on, keys in hand, and door open, you come to a realization: You really don't know the best place to go to actually purchase a koi. You sigh deeply, close the door, put your keys down, and take the coat off.

Even before you choose your individual koi, you're faced with the decision of *where* to purchase your fish. Luckily for you, koi fish have gained a newfound level of popularity that they never had in the past. Because of this, you have many options available to you.

Koi can be found in many retail outlets, pet stores, and even some garden centers. And that's in addition to the more traditional outlets such as individual breeders and koi farms.

Be careful when making your choice. Don't be shy about asking for references. Ask many questions and, if at all possible, visit the store or supplier prior to actually making the purchase.

Whatever you do, don't rush. I know that you want nothing more right now than to get a koi and put it in your new aquarium. But as you continue with this hobby, you'll quickly discover the value of taking your time. Find an honest and reputable seller, and then start deciding which particular koi you want.

The person you buy your koi from will become your valued friend. He or she will not only be advise you, but will also provide tips and advice for raising your fish once you've brought it home.

Choosing Koi

Now you try to figure out how to select the perfect koi for you. Luckily, all you need to do is review this portion of the book. I'll help guide you along if you've never purchased a koi (or any fish) before. And if you *have* adopted koi prior to this, hopefully you'll find a few pointers you either forgot about or never knew.

Your first consideration, of course, is your budget. Just as koi come in an array of colors and sizes, they also come in a variety of price ranges.

As you choose, you'll need to walk a tightrope of sorts. You don't want to get a "deal" on your koi by purchasing your new fish from a friend of a friend of a…well, you get the idea. On the other hand, if you're new to the hobby and your pond is new, you don't want to get extravagant and spend a fortune, either.

After all, what happens if there's a problem with the pond you've failed to detect? If you place all your koi in one pond only to discover a big problem, you stand a very real chance of losing your entire new stock.

But ultimately, you're the only one who can determine what's the "right" amount of money to spend.

The Age-Old Question of Age

This is a never-ending debate among those who love koi: How old should your fish be when you buy it? Many experts and experienced hobbyists say you should only buy mature fish, and should never buy the young ones.

They say that when you buy a young koi, you're never quite sure about the eventual quality of the markings. As a koi ages, sometimes its markings fade. Just as often, they say the markings may improve with age. Which way will that young fish go? Only time will tell.

In choosing this gorgeous fish for your aquarium or pond, consider the ultimate health of the individual koi. Check the fish for any signs of infectious or parasitic disease (I describe symptoms in some detail in a later chapter -- that should help you.)

For the most part, though, you'll be looking for holes in the fins, missing scales, or scales which have grown back, but not very well as well as bent fin rays. You'll also want to make sure the koi you finally select are free from curvature of the spine and any problems with the eyes.

Questions for
the Breeder

Once you're satisfied the fish are healthy, it's time to ask the breeders or the pet store staff some questions.

Ask about the background of the fish they have for sale. How long have they had them?

When they first received the fish, did they dip and quarantine the fish as recommended? (Yep, you'll learn about that in a later chapter as well!)

Even ask about any other fish they may have in that same tank system. Check their health.

If you're interested in a specific fish, many breeders will allow you to observe them "up close and personal." They'll place the fish in a light-colored container so you can fully inspect them. If a breeder offers, you should accept.

By the time you've completed reading this book, you'll have a good idea of what you're looking for. And if you don't, then take a friend who is knowledgeable in koi with you.

Don't Make This Mistake

Never, ever lift the koi directly from the water into the air via a net. The resulting damage from this action is likely to injure the fish.

Instead, tip them gently into a pan-shaped container that is already partially submerged into the water system. If the individual fish is too large and if the person handling it is skilled enough, then the fish may be lifted from the system by hand. But those are two big "ifs." It's always better to be safe than sorry. (I know it's a cliché, but it's a cliché for a reason!)

While you have the fish close to you, carefully and deliberately examine its flesh. Touch it. It should feel firm and its body should be symmetrical. And yes, the koi should even feel slightly slimy.

You don't want a fish that is either too dry

or one that has too much mucus on its scales. Either of these conditions, by the way, could be caused by sub-standard water quality.

So you're watching the fish interact, but what exactly are you looking for? First, you need to know that koi are social creatures. If you've never owned fish before, you may find it difficult to believe. I know I did at first. But think about it: most fish swim in groups. (Remember? You learned about those *schools of fish* in grade school!)

You're looking first for a social animal (not to be confused with a party animal!). If you're drawn to one but it seems off by itself, a loner if you will, you might want to choose a different one.

Beyond the Aquarium

Check out the fish's surroundings. Steer your focus beyond the pond. The general environment should be neat and clean. In the water itself you don't want to encounter any dead or dying fish.

And while you're scrutinizing the surroundings, ask a few general questions about the food these koi are eating and request their feeding schedule.

Make a few judgments as you go along. For example, do you get the general impression that this breeder really cares for the fish? Or is he or she just out to make a fast buck?

The Real Koi

Once you've satisfied yourself that the koi from this particular breeder are healthy, you can move on to the second part of the selection process -- finding the koi that suits your personal tastes.

I can't help but bring in some professional opinions here from watching the judging at fish shows. Of course, whether you want a fish up to show standards is entirely up to you. But even if you don't, it's still good to know what's expected of the fish.

Judges at these events use a precise scale upon which to judge their fish contestants. Basically, though, it all comes down to four main criteria.

Morphology of Koi

The first is called morphology. (Don't get

too excited -- your fish isn't going to morph into a transformer.) All morphology refers to is the body shape of the animal and how it conforms to the standard in the breed.

Unlike just about every other ornamental fish including goldfish, the koi is expected to fit into an "ideal" standard of symmetry. The shape of your ideal koi is actually a fusiform torpedo shape, and it's really quite pleasing to look at. The head is evenly tapering from the neck.

Born in the USA:
How to Tell

Ironically, in many instances you can tell a koi bred in the United States. Their head may be too box-like or blunt. Female koi by the way, are also broader at the shoulders than their male counterparts.   They're also broader than the male further back through their flanks as well.

The paired fins -- the pelvic and pectorals -- must be identical in shape and size. For show-quality, there should not be any torn fins or evidence of previous tears. All healing needs to occur evenly and should be symmetrical.

The remaining unpaired fins -- the dorsal,

anal, and caudal -- should all be similarly arrayed. They should reveal no trailing edges, and should not possess any elongations.

This doesn't include the category we've just talked about, the butterfly koi, which is not recognized in the show world. The day may come when they are, but it certainly hasn't arrived yet.

Symmetrical Scales

The rows of scales should be not only even, but symmetrical as well. The Gin Rin, Doitsu and other mirror- or German-scaled koi are compared to that unreachable "perfect" ideal in this area.

Of course, if the scales have been removed for whatever reason and have grown back, they must be as similar as possible in shape, color, reflectivity, and insertion point to the original scales. The loss or re-growth of scales does not immediately disqualify a fish from competition.

If the fish has permanently scarred scales or if it has missing scales, though, then it may be disqualified.

It's also interesting to note that in the

shows, just about every grand champion (and every runner-up, for that matter) has been female. Male koi are slightly too thin, even at full size.

Color and Pattern

Second, notice just how intense the colors of the fish are. You'll also want to inspect the pattern.

Obviously, the colors should be bright. According to some people, the koi's pattern should "tell a story." I've never discovered exactly what story these patterns should reveal, but I've always looked for patterns that align themselves with the standard descriptions as closely as possible.

You're probably wondering how judges decide this category. Oh, they have their ways! Let's take the color red. If your fish has red and is in the show, the judges will take a good long look at it. It should be bright, for one thing -- like blood or a juicy ripe tomato.

And so it is with the color black. The fish should be as deep a black as possible. No mistaking any black spots with gray. Whites need to be a snowy clean white, not a dirty, drab gray. And the metallic sheen to your koi must be clean and shining brightly.

When deciding on the patterns, this is where several meanings evolve depending on what variety of fish you've chosen. An azuma -- lightning -- pattern was all the rage nearly 20 years ago. This made the Kohaku and the Sanke (which actually has three colors -- red, white and black) very popular.

The number and shapes of those islands of color and pattern are important and are quite evident when it comes to buying koi. Meaning, you'll feel it in pocket book!

Along those same lines, you want the color to be distinct, no "bleeding" as koi keepers say. Red is definitely red and black is noticeably black. The colors' "margins" as they are called, need to be distinct and obvious. You don't want someone looking at your koi trying to decide if it has a red mark or an orange one.

Definite Markings

You also want a very clear line where one color ends and another begins. The last thing a judge wants to see is fading -- or bleeding -- from one color to the next.

Small, indefinite markings or tiny dark specks are not viewed favorably.

The balance or distribution of that color and the pattern is also important. While you're looking at a koi, draw an imaginary line down the midline of it from above. Draw another imaginary line intersecting the first line roughly in its middle.

These are the four distinct quadrants of your koi. Using this exercise, you will be able to visualize what I'm about to talk about a little easier.

When assessing the distribution of color and of pattern of the koi, there really are no strict mathematical formulas. The best description I've ever heard comes from Grant Fujita.

"Each pattern has to be clean, clear and even," he explained. "The pattern should not have any small white spots, or opening in the pattern."

And there you have it.

The Pattern Depends on the Size of the Fish

The actual pattern -- and hence how it gets

judged -- is really dependent on the size of the fish. The larger the fish, the more you expect this pattern to be big and bold.

While you may not want to take such great pains in choosing a koi up to the grand standards, it's still good to know what makes a healthy, happy koi.

Of course, everything related to colors and patterns is important to different degrees, again depending on the classification of the fish. Body conformation is vital no matter what variety you choose.

The final decision-maker in this process is, of course, you. If you're happy with the coloratio, the pattern, the intensity of the color, and the overall pleasing appearance of the fish, then don't let anything stop you from making the choice of a healthy koi.

Did you find one you like? Oh, it's a fairly new addition? Well, it'll need to go through the standard quarantine procedure before you can even begin to think about bringing it home. More than likely, the breeder will allow you to place a down payment on the little tyke. Then all you need to do is wait for the completion of the quarantine period.

Separating the Boys

From the Girls

Yes, I know it can be rough when it comes to koi. Nobody dresses a girl koi in pink and a boy koi blue, darn it.

When koi are young, it really is difficult to tell the boys from the girls. This makes it difficult, then, if you're adopting your koi for breeding purposes. And even more difficult if you're not, and don't want to see little koi popping their heads up in your koi pond one day!

As your fish age, however, you'll have an easier time in this area. They'll blossom, mature, and develop into the roles. Definite identification becomes not only possible, but as you learn more, a little easier as well.

You'll also want to determine your koi's sex if you're planning on showing it. I mentioned earlier that, for the most part, the females are usually the champions at show events.

Male koi, for the most part, are slender, compact, and very much "torpedo-like" in their general appearance. They have trim lines and smooth body contours.

Male koi actually behave differently than females, especially when they get in a group with other males. They are much more prone to dart about energetically and sharply. They turn abruptly -- and turn with great speed. Some owners even think they're "strutting," because they tend to display an attitude while they do this.

Males also have a skittish nature, and not just in their movements. This may sound a bit outlandish, but they seem to have an innate distrust of female koi. (I told you it was strange sounding!) Whether this behavior is distrust or just shyness it is a topic many koi owners argue about. But the male's skittish attitude extends to other areas as well.

Watch the next time you feed your koi. You'll probably see all the females clamoring for food. The males tend to hang back and take quite a bit longer to feed at the surface.

Physically, the key feature of male koi is latent development. They usually aren't ready for breeding until late spring. About this time, breeding nodules -- or bumps --

appear on the heads, flanks, and tails of the mature male broodfish. Very often these are mistaken for whitespot.

If you touch the bumps, you'll feel that they are even slimier than the rest of the koi body.

In koi with darker colorations, the nodules are usually white and clearly visible. On those varieties that are light colored or metallic, the nodules may not be seen, only felt.

In contrast, females don't develop any nodules. But don't expect them to keep those sleek body lines as the breeding season approaches. The ovaries of the females are filling with eggs -- and that causes a swelling in the abdomen.

Not only that, but you can tell a female koi from her behavior. She's nowhere near as shy or timid as the male of the species. You'll also notice that's she's one voracious eater! (And who wouldn't be, when you're eating for so many?)

How Can You Tell
For Sure?

Sure, all this observational information is

fine and dandy, you say. But you want to know for absolute fact if Kandy Koi is female, or else you'll have to start calling her Karl Koi!

The truth is, the only sure method of sexing koi is to examine them physically. So get ready to roll up your sleeves and exert some pressure in just the right place….

Your water has to be warmer than 15 degrees Celsius. If it is, then your male koi are producing **milt**, a substance which contains sperm.

To learn whether a particular koi has milt, simply apply your finger and thumb to the sides of the vent. You should be able to see it.

To identify a female, turn her upside down. (I suggest you sedate her first!) If the koi is female, she'll have a swollen abdomen and a pink, fleshy protruding vent.

If you have a pond and the room and it doesn't bother you, then you may be fine allowing your fish to flock spawn. But just be sure that you have fewer males than females when you do this.

I said males are timid, and they are. But

when in the presence of that perfect female koi, things change. The male really doesn't want any other fish around. (How romantic!) To prove this, the male will chase other fish away if he suspects the interloper is a male also ready to breed.

The best way to handle this situation is by giving the males more females. This means they have to divide their attention among all the females present. And this keeps everyone relatively happy.

If you want a concise checklist to help you remember the important points of choosing your koi, turn to Appendix III. I've created The Ultimate Koi Checklist. This provides you with a list of all the right questions to ask and all the proper items to examine before you set your money down on the table.

Now that you've found the perfect Kerry Koi, you're ready to bring it home. If you've never owned a fish before, you're about to be surprised….

Chapter 3:
Bringing Your Bundle of Koi Home

If you've never adopted a fish before or kept an aquarium, then you may be a bit skeptical about all this talk of "quarantines."

That's understandable, but seriously, it's not just talk. Quarantine -- though it sounds like a word out of the 17th century -- is a 21st century practice for koi keepers.

It has proven to be a very valuable practice again and again. I could give you a million reasons why. But instead, let me just tell you two short (fish) tales about why it may be one of the most important steps you take as a responsible koi owner.

Fish Tale #1

Mary Margaret O'Malley buys her koi from a local pet store. The pet store's quality of fish is rather questionable. What Mary didn't know when she bought her first koi was that it had a small infestation of an infection which was contracted from a goldfish. The two shared the same filtration system.

Mary, being relatively new to koi keeping

and extremely trusting, places her koi directly into her pond, which already has several other koi.

No more than a week later, Mary notices that some of her fish have patches of irritated scales. Specifically, the new koi she just bought has a red ulcer and is separating itself from the group.

Mary, although new to the hobby and trusting in her purchase, is still wise enough to know when she needs to consult a veterinarian. And she already has one she uses regularly. The vet stops by the pond.

After much struggle, she's able to get the sick fish out of the pond. He discovers the cause of the infestation and treats it. Everyone survives -- even Mary!

Yes, this story has a happy ending… eventually. But Mary could have avoided the story in the first place -- as well as the cost of treating the fish, the vet bill, and the stress involved -- had she simply quarantined the new arrival from the start.

Fish Tale #2

Now meet Mark Munro. Mark buys a koi. He buys it from a local breeder, thinking

he'll get a disease-free fish. But being a
veteran koi keeper, he also knows to expect
the unexpected.

He brings Kathy Koi home and places her in
the quarantine tank. Before he releases the
fish, he gives it a quick scrape to get a
specimen he can check out under a
microscope. He realizes the koi has a
parasite. Mark administers the proper
treatment, keeping the koi in the quarantine
tank for the rest of the period. Nearly a
month later, Kathy Koi is as healthy as can
be swimming with all the other koi.

The Need To Quarantine

I could lecture you on the value of
quarantining your new koi, but I'd rather
just show you. Let me tell you just how you
go about quarantining your new fish and for
how long.

Every new koi you introduce into your pond
or aquarium should be quarantined. It
needs to be kept separate for a minimum of
three to four weeks.

When you introduce a new individual into
your stock, you really don't know much
about its history. You don't know where it's

been, or what types of germs, bacteria, or other small critters it's been in contact with.

Worse yet, you really don't know what other fish your new bundle of koi might have come in contact with. And what types of menacing creatures and diseases they may have been exposed to, or even if they're carrying any overt symptoms of diseases themselves.

And that's why quarantining your new stock is so very important. For the most part, this quarantine period is just a precautionary measure. You may never actually encounter a problem with a new fish you've introduced to the social network.

But then again, do you really want to bet every koi you own on the newcomer's health status? I never wanted to take that chance.

Stress-Related Problems

Many of the problems koi parents find are related more to stress than to anything else. Imagine the amount of stress you would be under if someone placed you in a plastic bag and toted you home with them, then dumped you in an environment with complete strangers.

And then there's the divergent water conditions the koi may be exposed to during this process.

Right there, we have an effective recipe for a lowering of the fish's immune system. Under stress, this otherwise healthy fish is more vulnerable to parasites and bacteria than it normally would be.

Getting Comfy!

One of the major dangers of bringing a new koi home is the difference in water. In some instances, the temperatures can be as much as 15 degrees Celsius off from one destination to another. And this change in temperature occurs quickly, within a 24-hour period. That would give anyone stress!

You're far ahead of the game if you treat the problem before it occurs. Try to make the koi as comfortable as possible in its new home as quickly as possible. This helps to shield its immune system.

Build It, and
They Will Come

To be more exact, build the quarantine

aquarium and then use it! If you've never set up a quarantine aquarium or tank before, you're probably wondering how to accomplish this simple task. That's the new koi parent's first question. And it's not only a good question, it connotes a sense of responsible curiosity.

What you need for the quarantine tank depends in large part on the number of fish you expect to quarantine at any one time.

If you're quarantining only a few fish, then some people use only a clean, 55-gallon new garbage can.

If you're quarantining many fish at the same time, then consider using a 100-gallon aquarium -- or larger. Of course, the more fish you need to quarantine, the larger the tank you'll need.

Here is a list of the equipment and items you'll need to successfully set up your quarantine area:

Water.

Well, obviously. But the water you use should be fresh and contain no chlorine. It can be well water or – for best results – water from your pond.

Small filter and pump.
Heater.
Small air pump.
Waterproofed thermometer.
Net cover for tank.

Salt.

Wait. Don't reach for that table salt. You want the variety that does not contain iodine or YPS. You can use salt that comes with your water softener as long as it says it's 99.9 percent pure.

Scale.

You'll use this to weigh your fish.

Fluke tabs.

The fluke is a type of parasite which many koi have.

Ammonia binder.

Examples of these include Amquel and Prime.

Net.

This needs to be large enough to actually

hold the fish you purchase.

Okay, so now you've got all your ducks in a row when comes to equipment and supplies. Or to keep in the spirit of the hobby -- all your *koi* in a row!

Before you purchase additional koi, it's best to have the equipment all set up and running. Check the pH balance of the tank and ensure that it's between 7 and 7.5 If it's too low, you can add baking soda to bring the number up.

Should you have a pH balance of greater than 7.5, don't worry. You fish will easily adjust to that.

Before you place any fish in the quarantine tank, make sure that the temperature is roughly 78 degrees. If it isn't, then use the heater on your list.

Don't Let the Fish
Out of the Bag

Once you bring your new arrivals home, you'll want to allow them to float *in the bag* in the quarantine tank. Don't open the bag yet. Allow the fish to remain like this for 20 to 30 minutes.

Of course, there are a few exceptions to this rule. If the fish has already spent a great deal of time in the bag and is showing signs of stress, and if the difference in temperature in tank water is negligible, then the wisest move may be to skip this floating step all together. You may want to place the fish directly into the quarantine tank.

The water in the shipping bag undoubtedly carries a low pH balance, ultimately protecting the fish. The lower the pH, less toxic the ammonia in it is.

If you do continue on with the half hour of "in-bag" floating time, then carefully remove the fish from the bag after the time is up and place it in the quarantine tank.

Do not simply pour it into its new, temporary home straight from the bag, water and all. Instead, use a net that fits its size, retrieve the fish, and add it to the water. Don't pour the shipping water into your quarantine tank.

Yes, there's a very good reason for this. The original water may actually contain a multitude of bad bacteria, and even some fish feces. It's the equivalent of drinking from a total stranger's glass. You wouldn't do that, would you? So don't put a total stranger's water into your quarantine pond or aquarium.

In the Next…
12 Hours

Your job is done…at least for the next 12 hours. After 12 hours, you'll want to start adding salt. You'll need about a pound of salt for every 100 gallons of tank water.

The safest way to perform this job is by testing the water with a salt test kit after the first batch of the salt has been added. Give it enough time to not only dissolve, but also circulate through the water. Your kit should measure the salt level at about 0.10 percent. If you don't get a reading like that, you may have to add more.

Wait another 12 hours. Now it's 24 hours after you've added your fish to the quarantine tank. Test for ammonia and nitrite. Remember, while the fish are in the quarantine tank, there is absolutely no acceptable level for either of these.

If you should detect ammonia, you need to add either Amquel or Prime to counteract it. These products will not remove the ammonia, but they bind it in order to render it harmless to your fish. And that makes everybody happy.

What About Feeding A Quarantined Fish?

Depending on where you purchased your fish, you may have a very hungry animal on your hands. (Er, in your quarantine tank, that is.)

Did you say you brought it home from a koi show? Well then the chances are very good that it has not eaten in a few days – possibly even a week. Fish sold at shows are put on a fast (I doubt they readily agreed to this!) so they don't contaminate the water.

If, on the other hand, you've purchased your koi through a dealer, the little guy probably hasn't fasted.

When To Start Feeding The New Arrivals

Start feeding these quarantined fish after they're been in the tank for six to eight hours. But only give them a small amount of food. Keep feeding them in this manner for a while. Don't worry about feeding them enough; it's better for them to eat two smaller portions of food twice a day than one larger portion only once a day.

Don't worry if the fish don't eat this food right away. It's not uncommon for fish to avoid eating while they're adjusting to new surroundings.

The newly acquired fish may also hide for a few days while getting accustomed to their new home. This is hardly the basis for concern. After several days, they begin to feel more at home and eventually come out of hiding.

You may want to help your fish "hide" by floating a piece of Styrofoam on top of the water. This gives it a place to hide. This isn't without its dangers, though. More than one small fish has jumped, landed on the Styrofoam, and died. For this reason, use small pieces of Styrofoam. This way the little guy (or gal!) can easily flop over and get back into the water.

When you buy the fish, some dealers also supply you with several days' worth of food. The fish are used to eating this food. Most parents of koi say that a new fish adjusts better -- and stays healthier -- if its menu is the same as it was in its old home.

Pay close attention to your new koi for at least the first week that it's in the quarantine tank. After the addition of fish to the tank, it's common to detect nitrate in it, and nitrate poisons your fish.

Specifically, nitrate poisoning interferes with the fish's ability to intake oxygen. It actually causes the blood to run brown. And yes, it is fatal if not treated. One of the safeguards, however, is the salt you already added to the tank. In many instances, this ingredient keeps the nitrate out of the fish's system.

If you consult some koi parents about this scenario, they may advise you to change the water in your quarantine aquarium. I disagree with them. If it will make you feel better, you can change about 10 percent of the water once a week. But I really don't recommend any more than that.

Making that drastic of a change only slows down the nitrogen process. You'll soon learn that even with an 80 percent water change, the ammonia or the nitrite level rushes back to the "pre-change" days.

Large, wholesale changes in water are just

downright stressful to the fish. And fish in a quarantine situation, particularly the new arrivals, are already stressed out enough.

Viruses in the Quarantine Tank

It happens. And that's the very real reason you're placing your fish in a quarantine tank first. What am I talking about? The appearance and spread of viruses.

Two very common viruses which you need to monitor your new fish for are the SVC and the Koi Herpes Virus, often times referred to as KHV. Many owners have lost entire koi ponds because they skipped the quarantine step when introducing their new fish.

Realistically, if your new arrivals have either of these viruses, you may lose them. But at least you still have a pond full of beautiful, healthy fish if you've taken the time and effort to quarantine the sick fish.

The sad truth is that there is no cure for these two viruses. It's possible that if your new fish are infected, they may still survive. But the bad news is that if they do live, they are now carriers of those viruses. Even though they aren't overtly sick at moment, they can pass this virus on to others in the pond.

The virus is triggered by heat, so you'll want to raise the temperature in the quarantine tank. Turn it up to at least 78 degrees. In a temperature any cooler than this, the virus lies dormant in the fish's system. Once the water warms, though, the viruses strike.

If you find that your new fish do have the viruses, they should be destroyed. Then you should use a bleach solution to clean the entire quarantine system, including the filter and anything else that came in contact with the fish. This includes all the nets and all the tubs.

When Can the Guys "Bust Out"?

So just how long do you keep your new fish in the quarantine tank? After all, they can't live in there forever. There are probably as many answers to this question as there are koi parents.

My personal opinion -- as koi parent to many, many fish -- is not less than three weeks. Personally, I quarantine all my new arrivals for a minimum of 30 days. During this time I check on them daily.

Other koi parents say you should keep them in the separate tank for a minimum of six weeks, and some even say eight. Ultimately, you have to make that decision for yourself.

Let me remind you that that a proper quarantine procedure isn't solely about keeping the new fish separate. That's surely a large part of it, but during this period, you should also be monitoring your new fish. You can also be checking for parasites. No, you really don't need a microscope. I've included a chapter later in the book on exactly how to spot these nasty critters.

The Most Common Quarantine Mistakes

Think you've got this quarantine procedure down? Maybe you have. Below are some of the most common mistakes owners make when it comes to bringing baby home and placing it in a separate tank. Why not stack your performance up against these common mistakes?

Not measuring.

You just can't place a fish in the quarantine tank for a month without monitoring and measuring the ammonia and nitrite levels of the water. You must do this.

And just for the record, I'll tell you again. Any trace of ammonia or nitrate is not acceptable. Any at all!

Not watching the fish closely enough.

One of the very reasons you place your new koi in this temporary home is so you can monitor it closely. You really undo all your hard preparation work if you walk away on day two or three and don't show up again until day thirty or so.

This time is dedicated to examining the fish closely for parasites. In this period, you also must keep the fish's water as clean as possible. And as you already know, that means no ammonia and no nitrate.

Too small of a tank.

This sounds like a no-brainer, but it's important: make sure that your tank is big enough.

No netting on your tank.

The experts tell us this over and over again, but we never think it's going to happen to us. A fish that has been moved is a very good candidate for jumping. It is more likely to jump from the tank itself. And once you place it in the pond, it's apt to jump out of that, too.

After several days, the koi will settle down. It's just the unfamiliar surroundings making it behave this way. That's why it's a great idea to put netting over the tank when you bring your new fish home.

So how did you do? Have you committed any of these common mistakes? Probably not. You're well on your way to becoming a committed, conscientious, and caring koi keeper.

Congratulations!

Next, we're tackling the fundamentals of feeding koi. We'll not only talk about commercial food and the practice of feeding your fish "people food," but we'll also talk about nutrition, too!

Chapter 4:
Koi Nutrition

S o you've brought Kerry Koi home, and the entire family is excited about her. (Or him; you might not be quite sure yet!) But you still have one small detail ahead of you. What exactly does the new member of the family eat?

Koi food. Excellent answer. And yes, you can feed her commercial food. But in order to discover which type of a commercial diet is best for her, you may want to know a little more about her nutritional needs.

The koi fish, like every other living thing, has its own unique dietary needs. But while its needs may be unique, we'll talk about them in terms that you can easily understand.

The koi body requires all the same nutrient groups that your body craves and needs for healthy functioning. Why don't we start with a familiar category: proteins.

The Koi Need
For Protein

The younger the koi, the more protein the fish need. That's an excellent rule of thumb to follow. Fry -- what the baby koi are called -- require diets that contain 37 to 42 percent protein.

Compare this to adult koi whose protein needs are only 28 to 42 percent of their total diets.

But there's more to this than just the amount. Many experts feel that there are better times of the year to feed your fish protein than other times.

The theory behind this is that this particular nutrient is difficult for the fish to break down (at least relative to all the other nutrients they eat). They recommend that koi eat less protein during the colder months of the year.

That doesn't mean you should withhold protein altogether from your koi. Never allow its protein consumption to drop below 28 percent of its total diet. This results in a deficiency.

Lipids Needs

You may not be as familiar with the term *lipids* as you are with its synonym, fats. Fats, as you recall from your health class, supply your body with energy. They do the very same thing for your fish. And they are extremely important for the internal organs and the cells of the fish's body.

As a koi parent, you need to walk a fine tightrope when it comes to feeding your fish fats. If you give your koi too many foods rich in saturated fat, like pork, beef or even poultry, you're not helping its health.

Just like our health, the health of a koi depends on it receiving an adequate supply of unsaturated oils. Most of the commercial koi food on the market today contains the proper amount, between five to eight percent fat.

If you feed your koi too much more fat than that, it'll gain weight. Not only that, but fat deposits begin to form.

Too few fats or lipids can have undesirable results on the body as well. If the koi doesn't get enough fat, not only does it experience fin erosion, but it could develop heart problems as well.

If you plan on feeding your new fish commercially prepared food, then make sure you purchase those products especially produced for koi -- and only koi.

There are many other foods that are created just for trout, or salmon, or even catfish. While they're great for the species they were developed for, they aren't healthy for your koi. Don't ever buy them as a substitute for your koi food!

Carbohydrates

Carbohydrates are another vital source of energy. Most food sold through pet stores contains a lot of carbohydrates. Examples of carbohydrates include wheat, rice, barley, and corn.

At one time, it was thought that the koi had no problems digesting this nutrient group. Popular thought is now shifting. Experts are just discovering that koi don't digest carbohydrates well after all.

For this reason, avoid foods that contain an abundance of cereals. And this is why you must be careful what types of household foods you offer to your colorful carp. Don't feed them foods like bread, breakfast cereals, or even dog biscuits.

Vitamins

We've all heard of vitamins. They're the building blocks for proper metabolism.

You're probably familiar with many already. You can divide these nutrients into two camps: those that are water soluble and those that are fat soluble.

You'd be amazed just show many symptoms and ailments can be triggered through a vitamin deficiency, including loss of appetite, reduced growth, malformed bones, and even eye protrusion.

The best food sources of vitamins for koi are green plants, vegetables, fruit, liver, and believe it or not, fish oils. Basically, you can use all of these foods as supplements. In this way, you ensure your koi won't suffer from a vitamin deficiency.

Minerals

Tissue formation and metabolism. These are the two vital functions to which minerals contribute. And among the stars of the koi mineral show are calcium and phosphorous. Deficiencies in these two nutrients can reveal themselves in your koi as poor bone formation, slow growth, and a depressed appetite.

Food sources for these two crucial minerals include spinach, kale, and lettuce. And here's a hint when choosing lettuce: the greener the leaves, the more nutrients it contains!

Choosing Food

Now that we've covered a general overview of koi nutrition, it's time to talk about the kinds of foods available to you and your koi.

Four categories exist: commercially prepared foods, frozen or freeze-dried food, live food, or household foods.

Surprisingly, the most harmful to your fish is the live food choice. While this may seem like the option that provides the best nutrition, it contains a hidden danger. Feeding your fish live food exposes them to all the potential diseases and parasites that live food may be carrying.

Commercially Prepared Foods

This category of food has your koi nutrition covered. When you feed your fish prepared foods you've bought from the pet store, you can be sure that it contains the basics ingredients of sound nutrition.

In addition, you have the peace of mind of knowing that this food is also supplemented with the necessary vitamins and minerals.

You'll find commercially prepared koi foods in a variety of forms. The most common is as pellets. Popular with owners, pellets are tossed into the water where they sink or float, depending on the brand you buy. And you can purchase them in a variety of sizes.

The popularity of the floating pellet is understandable. Many owners say they prefer these pellets because it gives them a chance to watch the fish feed on the surface of the water. This allows them to easily and effectively monitor their fish's diets.

The sinking variety of pellets comes with several disadvantages. When the pellets sink to the bottom of the tank, several problems may occur. Not only is it more difficult to monitor what the fish are eating, but they can compromise the quality of your tank or pond water.

Choosy Koi Parents
Choose...

Don't select just *any* commercially prepared koi food. First, you must be sure that the food is prepared for koi -- and only koi. The nutritional needs of koi are different from other species of fish. While you think fish food is fish food is fish food...surprise! Not all fish food is created equal.

The truth of the matter is that commercially prepared food is really only a foundation of a healthy diet. It's an excellent foundation, but your fish will really thrive if you build on it.

The only way to do that is to give your fish dietary supplements to create and maintain a balanced nutritional health plan. And as with commercially prepared food, the supplements you administer to your fish should be strictly for koi only. You should not be giving your koi supplements created for any other species.

You don't need to worry about where you're going to find these koi supplements. The vast majority of pet stores stock them.

By the way, you should carefully store your commercially prepared koi food if you want to maintain its quality. Heat and moisture harm the food. Store it in cool, dry area.

Never buy more than a 90-day supply of food. After 90 days, the food loses much of its nutritional qualities. Similarly, don't leave the container open and exposed to the air or it loses its integrity. The same goes for your fish's dietary supplements.

Vitamins, too, are sensitive to temperatures. If you store them in an area where the temperature is too high, the ingredients break down.

Live Foods

Some owners feed their koi live food. On the surface, this sounds like an excellent choice. It certainly is the best method of ensuring your fish are receiving top notch nutrition.

But this method also contains some hidden dangers which I alluded to earlier. Many koi experts and long-time keepers refuse to feed their fish this type of food. They say the risk that the live food may be carrying disease is too great.

Others, though, have overcome that pitfall by taking a simple precaution: they buy their live food from a dealer or pet store. Not only is this safer, but it's much more convenient than collecting live specimens from a pond or a lake.

Your Koi, Its Diet,
And Its Color

The color of your fish is largely dictated by

his genetic makeup. That's a fact. But the koi's color is also affected by the water in your pond as well.

Did you know that what your fish eats can also impact your koi's colors? It's true! Want to enhance the color of your fish? You can purposely alter its diet to make its colors even more remarkable.

Let me give you just a small indication of what a diet can do for your koi. Take shrimp, marigold, plankton, and even the blue-green algae known as Spirulina. They have all been added to your commercially prepared foods specifically to enhance color.

If you opt to feed your koi frozen or freeze-dried foods, you're choosing foods with certain color-enhancing ingredients. Included in this category of food are ingredients like brine shrimp and daphnia. Each of these carries high concentrations of carotenoid pigments. These are the major pigments of the koi's skin.

Too Much
Of a Good Thing

And it's precisely for this reason you must be careful when you feed your fish. There is indeed a moment when you -- or in this instance your koi -- can get too much of a good thing.

Some fish on commercial diets may receive too much pigment. If you have any koi that are predominantly white, you'll need to be doubly sure you don't feed them too much. And if by chance you do, then simply reduce the amount of color-enhancing food they eats. It's really very simple.

What About
People Food?

Many people unfamiliar with this species of fish are surprised to learn that it's perfectly all right to feed your fish "people food." Of course, I should qualify this.

For starters, there are indeed some foods that we eat that koi could also eat and benefit from. Some of these foods include fresh, frozen, or canned oysters, clams, mussels, crabmeat, and lobster. (Who ever had leftover lobster?)

Other foods you may be startled to learn that koi like -- and are actually good for them -- include baked or boiled beans, steamed cauliflower and broccoli, and baked or boiled potatoes (hold the butter and sour cream, please!).

Spinach or lettuce also makes good additions for your koi.

Don't let these guys fool you, though. They'll eat just about anything. And "just about anything" includes beef, boneless chicken, and pasta. But if you decide to feed these items to your koi, feed them only in moderation.

The reason to feed koi additional foods is really just to augment their skin color. These foods were never intended to be their main diet.

Getting Down To Business:
Feeding Your Fish

If you're like I was when I bought my first koi, you're baffled by how you're supposed to feed these guys. How can you tell when enough is enough?

The first several sessions may leave you feeling a little baffled and more than a little concerned about whether you've fed your little guys enough. But trust me, before long you'll be feeding your koi like an old pro.

Keep in mind that between your feedings,

your fish won't starve. They spend the majority of their day foraging -- looking for and eating algae, insects, and plants that make their way to the pond.

If you adhere to the following guidelines, you'll have a good sense of what to feed your koi.

1. Provide your fish as much food as they can eat within five minutes.

2. Within that five minutes of feeding, only give them small portions.

3. If you're home, the best way to feed your fish is to spread their feeding times throughout the day -- as long as you provide them with only small portions.

4. If you're not home, then feed your fish twice a day. Make sure it's as close to the same times every day as possible. Give them only small portions. And if you have young koi, they need to be fed even more times than this.

5. In addition to feeding your fish at about the same times, feed them in the same general area of the pond as well.

6. Don't overfeed the fish. The act of overfeeding can stress out your fish and help to deplete their immune systems. Overfeeding also causes small particles of rock or other materials to accumulate, which decrease the quality of the water.

7. Monitor all of your fish while you're feeding them. Make sure that each of your fish gets their fair share of food. If a fish doesn't have an appetite, monitor it. This is often the initial signal of an impending ailment.

8. Start your koi with commercially prepared food. As your koi get adjusted to their environment, then you can add a variety of foods. *Don't crumble the food before you give it to them.* This adds to the degradation of the water. Your fish won't have any trouble chewing and grinding the whole pelleted foods themselves.

9. Remove as much uneaten food as possible. You don't want this food hanging around, literally decomposing in your pond.

What and how you feed your new koi are vital to its long-term health. But, as we're about to see if the next chapter, there are several other factors that determine just how happy (and healthy) you koi can be.

Chapter 5:
Koi Care

G ot a pond? Think it's perfect for koi? You might be right. Just remember that koi need not only a large area, but an area with enough depth as well. And there's really no reason that if your pond is aldedy dense with pond plants, you can't make your koi feel right at home there.

These fish, even though they are social animals, will do their best if the total population is kept small, with lots of room to roam. You've heard the phrase "a big fish in a little pond." Well, these guys like to be big fish in a big pond -- and the fewer their neighbors, the better.

In fact, as you decide on how many koi your pond can hold, keep the following rule of thumb in mind: You shouldn't stock more than one inch of fish for every square foot of pond surface area you have.

The other crucial item every koi owner should know, especially new keepers, pertains to the ammonia level. Monitor your water closely and keep a watchful eye on the amount of ammonia in your water.

Algae Alert

Ah, algae! The potential nightmare of every pond owner. But it really doesn't have to be. Controlling the buildup of algae in your pond is much easier than you think.

You have two different approaches from which to choose. You can go the natural route or you can choose to control the algae through chemical means.

Most pond owners use a combination of the two methods. Of course, because you're trying to maintain the quality of your fish as well as of your plants, your ultimate goal is for a natural balance.

After all, your pond is a natural ecosystem in and of itself. In order to keep it running smoothly, several guidelines need to be maintained.

First, when I talk of chemical control (or other koi parents talk about it), I'm referring to the use of *algaecides*. This is a class of chemicals that kills -- or at the very least inhibits -- all types of algae to some degree.

These chemicals normally include a variety of ingredients, not the least of which are simazine, chelated copper, and potassium permanganate.

You don't need to worry about the chelated copper. This doesn't harm vascular plants. It may, however, inhibit the growth of hyacinths or of plants that get their nutrients straight from the water.

If you use too much of any product containing chelated copper, you may end up killing your fish unintentionally. Products with simazine will inhibit the growth of most water plants as well.

Dying Algae
and Ammonia

These chemicals are used by many of us as a preventive measure. It's much better never to have algae at all than to have it grow and have to kill it.

And I'm just not talking about the time and effort expending on eliminating the algae. There's one more factor to take into consideration when killing off the algae: the increase in ammonia the dying algae create while at the same time depleting the oxygen.

If you allow the algae to build up and then have a "massive" killing of it, you can set your pond up for disaster. While the algae is decomposing, ammonia is being released and the oxygen supply is shrinking. This may ultimately result in dead fish.

It's better to use the algaecides *before your pond turns green.*

It's as Thick as
Pea Soup Algae

Is your pond plagued by planktonic algae? You may also know it as "pea soup" algae. If you have it, then you definitely want to find a sure-fire way of eliminating it. You can do this easily enough with water-clarifying chemicals. These chemicals pose no threat to your fish or your plants. And that's cool! Some chemicals that fall into this category include Rapid Clear, Microblift AquaRem, and Pond Clear Powder.

Ultimate Goal:
A Natural Balance

Your primary overriding goal is to strike a natural balance. The trick to controlling algae through natural means is twofold: you must limit the sunlight and nutrients that algae feed off of.

Algae require sunlight to survive. If your

pond is shallow -- less than 18 inches deep -- then this may prove difficult. The sunlight easily reaches the bottom.

Deep ponds are preferable in the well-lit garden. In the last chapter, I suggest building one that's no less than four feet in depth. It's much harder for the sun to penetrate through all that water to the bottom. Of course, if you already have a pond suitable for koi, you have to work with the depth you have.

If you can shelter your pond from sunlight, you can control the algae much easier. Creating some type of overhead structure is one method of limiting sunlight. Some owners take a 70 to 80 percent shade cloth and cover their entire pond with it.

Water Lilies:
More Than Beauty

The presence of water lilies in a pond helps to create shade. Your goal with plants like this is to achieve 70 percent plant coverage over the pond's surface.

Your next step is to remove the nutrients that algae need to live. Just like you and your koi need proper nutrients, algae require the same thing. Cut off their nutrients, and algae just won't thrive. It's that simple.

So what do algae thrive on? What are the nutrients they need to grow (and create an utter nuisance for you)? Look at this list:

- Fish waste
- Fish food
- Decaying algae
- Dead fish
- Leaves
- Debris
- Specific phosphates or nitrates in tap water

Even a good rain can leach some algae fertilizer into your pond. One would think it was an out-and-out conspiracy!

In order to remove the algae, you need to remove these items from your pond. This requires proper circulation throughout the entire system. The goal? To sweep debris into the drains.

Oh, did I forget to mention this? An excessive amount of debris can cause something called "string" algae. You'll want to remove large pieces of debris from feeding materials and from any other items decomposing in your pond.

Environmental Needs

As you may have already deduced from talking about the quarantine tank, koi have definite environmental needs. You can't just bring your fish home on the off chance it will adjust on its own. That just won't happen.

But that doesn't mean the koi's needs are impossible to meet; not by a long shot. A little loving care on your part, and your koi will be happy as…well, koi.

Look at any koi pond. Notice the plants. They aren't there for ornamental sake only, even though they're quite beautiful. They actually supplement your fish's diet.

I know you're already feeding them commercially prepared food and dietary supplements, but look at it this way. Koi still crave those "fresh greens." When they see those plants, koi view them as food too good to pass up. Grasses and submerged lilies -- who could ask for any better snacks? And they're available all the time. Koi heaven!

Koi Are Omnivores

Like their cousin, the wild carp, koi are omnivores. That means they eat meat and vegetables alike. Yep! Just like humans.

You may notice that your koi damage your plants. In addition to thinking they're the latest and greatest midnight snack, koi rummage through the plants searching for insects and larvae to eat. Vegetables and meat, all in one meal...delicious and well-balanced!

So if you want to keep valuable plants in your pond, place them in tubs before you put them in the pond. If you're using bricks as a platform for your plants, paint them. This prevents them from leeching lye into the pond water. The lye is toxic to your fish and gives your pond a dangerously high pH balance.

Not All Water
Is Created Equal

Some of us were not blessed with good water. Sometimes, out of necessity, we are even forced to use tap water. And in you didn't know, city water usually has a high pH level.

High pH levels, as I've mentioned, aren't good for koi. If you find that your tap water is high and you don't have another source of water, you may want to rethink the reasons you want koi. You may want to consider adopting some goldfish instead. No, I'm not being sarcastic.

Goldfish don't mind the higher pH level, and they come in a variety of colors and personalities. It's not that I'm trying to dissuade you from the koi, it's just that your water is naturally more inviting to the goldfish.

Now that you have some idea of what it takes to care for koi, you're ready to tackle the next logical topic: diseases. Diseases don't attack koi any faster or often than they attack other fish,   but being able to identify an ill koi as quickly as possible can help you quarantine it more quickly. And this may help you confine the spread of the disease or disorder through your pond.

Chapter 6:
Keeping Koi Disease-Free

Let's face it, there is no koi parent who doesn't want to keep his or her fish disease-free. After all, it hurts us to see these beautiful creatures suffering. It also worries and frightens us knowing that whatever disease one fish may have contracted can spread swiftly to the others.

Instead of just one ailing fish, you soon have a pond full of them. Depending on the severity of the disease and the circumstances surrounding it, there's the very real potential that you might lose your entire pond of beautiful, loving koi. It's not fair, and it's totally unnecessary.

So let's get busy. This is one of the most important chapters in this book. No matter how big a pond you have, no matter how great your water quality is, if you don't have healthy koi to enjoy, you don't have anything, do you?

Stress and
The Single Koi

Stress is now being increasingly implicated in many diseases that we, as human beings, contract -- from cancer to heart disease, and even sinusitis.

You may not be aware that stress is also a contributing factor to many of the diseases which affect your koi. And yes, stress works on the fish system much like it works on ours. It slowly, insidiously lowers your koi's immune system.

So exactly what does a koi have to be stressed about? You gaze into your pond thinking, *They certainly have the life. No bills to pay. No mortgage to worry about. No job to pressure them.*

True, but they do have pressures of their own. Their stress, in large part, comes from their physical environment. So you, as their loving koi parent, have a chance to help them live with as few stressors as possible.

Look at their environment: water. This may sound terribly silly because it's so obvious. Compare this to our environment: air. When do you feel better? When you breathe smoggy air polluted with untold toxins, or when you go to an environment in the country where the pollution is minimized?

The Quality of Water

Bingo! Now you understand the dire importance of *water quality* to your fish. Many of their stress-related problems arise from exposure to a poor quality of water.

But before I jump into that, let me explain just how stress can wreak havoc on your fish's system.

How Stress Affects Koi

When a fish first recognizes it is under stress, its body releases adrenalin, the same way we get a rush of adrenalin when we experience stress. The hormone gives the koi the strength and stamina it needs to make a quick getaway.

The release of this adrenalin is absolutely essential to the health -- and when predators are present, the life -- of your koi. But it doesn't occur without consequences.

For starters, the release of adrenalin can seriously and adversely affect the balance of salt and water in the pond ecosystem. And this in turn can seriously affect your fish's immune system.

Remember that mucus your koi produces? Its role is to create a physical barrier between the environment and your koi. It also establishes a barrier between the fish and parasites.

When the water conditions deteriorate, your fish produces more mucus. Adrenalin produces poor water conditions, which in turn, cause your fish to produce even more mucus.

This excessive mucus encourages the growth of parasites. In fact, two parasites in particular just love to munch on mucus: the **Costia** and the **Trichodina.**

Stress-Induced
Cortisol

But wait, I'm not quite finished yet! Let's go a step beyond this. The presence of stress also produces another hormone, cortisol. It's the same hormone we produce when we react negatively to a stressor in our lives.

Cortisol compromises the actions of your fish's immune system. Specifically, it hampers the ability of your fish to manufacture white blood cells, which are crucial to the health of its immune system.

This increases its vulnerability to disease and illness. It's a double whammy of potential ailments!

In an ideal pond world, the goal is to remove as many stressors as possible, as quickly as possible. This would mean eliminating the ammonia and nitrite in the water and improving the oxygen levels.

Of course, not all stressors come in the form of bad water. A bird or a cat might be lurking around the pond. The cat might have a fork and knife in its hand, waiting for just the right moment to grab dinner….

This would stress any fish out. If this is the case, eliminate the cat from the equation. (He'd be easy to identify -- he's the only cat wearing a napkin around his neck!)

Once the Stressor
Has Been Removed...

Once you've pinpointed and eliminated the cause of tension from the environment, be patient. It may take time for your fish's stress levels to return to normal. Until that occurs, your fish is still vulnerable to illness.

I'm about to break this down one step further for you. First, I'm going to talk briefly about the prevention of disease. Then, we'll talk about how to maintain the health of your koi.

This may sound like I'm splitting hairs (er, gills?), but the truth of the matter is, it's much easier for us to treat these as two distinct topics. In real life, the areas overlap. But you'll be able to better understand the problems when they're presented like this.

Koi Disease
and Water Quality

At this point, I don't think I need to convince you that disease and water quality (or lack thereof) go hand in hand. The following tests are among the most important you can run to help maintain your water quality. High-quality water will help *prevent your koi from developing disease.*

Make sure that the level of nitrate in your pond is no more than 50 ppm (parts per million).

Make sure you have no ammonia and nitrite in your pond.

Avoid a population explosion in your pond. Make sure you have a sensible fish load with a desirable stocking density. Did you know that fish actually grow faster in a pond in which the stocking density is lower? They bodies are simply reacting to the larger areas of water.

The lower the stocking rate, the less stress on the fish. You've reduced the competition among the koi during their feeding period. (I bet you didn't even realize they were competing!)

The Importance of a
Good Filtration System

Stress can be reduced through a quality filtration system. By keeping the water circulating properly, you maintain a higher level of quality with less chance of debris -- or bacteria -- build up. The absence of bad bacteria floating around means your koi are less likely to develop disease.

Don't forget about the importance of diet on your fish's stress level. I've already devoted an entire chapter to diet, especially the affect it has on the koi's stress levels and its overall health.

Whatever you do, don't beat yourself up. It's impossible to prevent all water-borne bacteria and other pathogens from sneaking into your koi pond. So when you find something, don't feel guilty. In fact, most of the time you should feel pretty good about yourself for keeping the pond as bacteria-free as it is.

The use of a UV sterilizer or clarifier helps to eliminate much of the bacteria, but your pond may still be harboring bacteria somewhere.

After all, consider this fact: It's possible for bacteria, viruses, fungus, and parasites to enter your pond's environment through the air. You're never going to provide your koi with a completely sterile environment or one which promises the elimination of all potential disease. We certainly don't live in a utopia like that.

Diseases of the Koi

There are several types of bacteria, parasite, fungi, and other illnesses common to koi. Some of these diseases are also common to other tropical fish. If you're a veteran around fish, then you may have heard of some these. If you're new to fish keeping altogether, then these diseases and illnesses may be new to you. Either way, it's great to get to know and review the symptoms, so you can quickly recognize them in your fish.

ICH

Sounds like an appropriate name for a disease! It's actually the abbreviation of an unpronounceable disorder called *Ichthyophthirius multifilis.*

And now it's abundantly clear why it's known simply as Ich. In freshwater fish, this disorder reveals itself through small spots on the bodies of the fish. In some instances you won't be able to see these spots without the use of a microscope.

The disease is caused by a ciliated protozoan. While it attacks all fish, the smaller fish are the ones most adversely affected. In many instances, the smaller fish don't survive.

It does its damage by attacking the gills. The life cycle of this parasite is only two to five days, although it has been known to hang out and make itself at home for as long as five weeks (yikes!) if the water is cool. The warmer the water, the shorter the length of time this guy lingers.

Knowing this, your first step in treating this problem is to turn up the heat. Then, add some salt to the water. This second treatment phase has the potential to harm your plants. You may want to find an alternative by talking to your veterinarian.

Chilodinella

If you're not familiar with the symptoms of this disorder, you need to learn them. This is one of the most common causes of fish death. If you view this organism under a microscope, it appears to be a distinct bean shape. You may also see a round organism full of what look like tiny bubbles.

If the particular organism you're viewing is alive, then it looks very much like a heart-shaped onion (if you can imagine such a thing), with a fuzzy end in the spot you would think roots should grow.

The fuzzy end is actually a group of dead cilia.

Chilodinella are actually motionless round balls. Those things that look like bubbles inside them -- they really are bubbles.

You may confuse these critters with Ich. They certainly look like the other parasite. But unlike Ich, chilodinella don't have a crescent nucleus, nor do they move when they're dead.

You can easily eliminate chilodinella with salt, but you have to leave the salt in the system for a good 14 days -- that's a full two weeks. While you have the salt in the pond, don't forget to run supplemental aeration. These organisms can cause gill damage in your koi, and sometimes it can be quite severe.

If you have a pond with a large number of fish dying on the surface, this disease should be your first thought. You should also think chilodinella if you have fish who roll over on their sides unless you disturb them. The koi themselves will often dash madly about when affected by this.

Costia or Ichthyobodo

With the uncanny capability to kill fish in great number, this parasite attacks the freshwater variety of koi. Costia may be attached or stuck onto the skin or gill of the fish. They look much like little commas.

When unattached, they are free-swimming creatures without much grace. They're wobbly things resembling half-open conch shells.

The good news about these parasites is that they are easily killed with the use of salt.

You should suspect costia when you have many fish dying, when the fins of your fish are reddened, or if you notice your fish aren't breathing well.

Fish dying of this disorder possess spider web-like lesions and an abundance of mucus on the skin.

Trichondina

Capable of causing spider-web lesions on your koi, the trichondian is a saucer-shaped parasite. While it's a nuisance, a hindrance, and definitely a stressor...it's seldom fatal.

For the most part, Trichondian cause mild damage to the gills of the smaller fish.

I'm not implying you can simply ignore these creatures. If nothing else, the presence of this parasite is your wakeup call that there is something amiss in your system. It's your signal to go find it and fix it.

Oodinium

The Velvet disease. Never heard of it? I'm

not too surprised. It's relatively rare. The oodinium produce a velvety, gold dust look to koi. It's more likely to strike goldfish.

Lernea

An anchor worm, the lernea elegans poses a real threat to koi. They attach onto the fish ventrally, and then they hold on tightly for about two weeks. After that, they start reproducing...and reproducing...and reproducing.

When they do this, they almost always cause harm to the koi through the ulcer disease bacteria, aeromonas. Now your problem has doubled, and quickly.

You can use salt to kill the free-swimming reproductive worms.

Argulus Lice

You'll know these guys when they strike. They're greenish and disc shaped, and they "suck" onto the fins and the sides of fish. They can damage the koi enough to cause ulcer formation.

Gyrodactylus

Never heard of it? Perhaps you've heard of a fluke. Well the fluke is a class of gyrodactylus. Among the flukes, there are two varieties: skin and gill.

But it really isn't necessary for you to be concerned which kind your fish have -- just knowing that it has them is concern enough. The presence of flukes cause flashing in koi (as well as several other species of fish).

The good news is that gyrodactylus are rarely fatal. They eat slime in addition to creating microscopic wounds on the gills and skin of koi.

These wounds become infected and, believe it or not, this secondary infection is actually worse than the invasion of flukes in the first place.

Flukes live about 14 days, but they are quite capable of completing a reproductive-maturation cycle in a mere four days. Now, you can see the problem!

Dropsy or
Bloater

Dropsy or bloater -- whatever you call it, it's the same problem. Some people even call it Pine Cone disease. It's usually caused by a bacterial invasion of the kidney.

Sometimes the presence of the herpes virus may contribute to it.

The bad news is that dropsy cannot be treated. There's even worse news though. By the time the major symptom -- protruding scales -- form on the body, the damage to the kidney has already occurred. Not only is the damage irreversible, it's usually fatal.

If you try to save the affected fish, isolate it first. Expose it to elevated water temperatures and increase its oxygen supply. Then begin injecting the fish with antibiotics.

Saprolegnia

Fungal infections which affect koi and other ornamental fish are most often caused by the saprolegnia. This is a common fungus. It seems to strike only when a stressor is present.

The most frequently affected fish are those koi keepers call "surviving jumpers." They are the ones who have jumped overboard, out of the pond, and have lived to tell their fellow pond-mates about it.

The ulcers garnered for whatever reason

often get infected with this fungus. The symptoms of the disease bear a resemblance to cotton-wool protruding from a lesion. It may become stained with algae.

The only way you can tell for sure if your fish has this infection is by looking under a microscope.

Scoliosis

This disorder can be caused by several different contributors, and you'll be relieved to hear that it's not infectious. For the most part, it's caused by a vitamin C deficiency.

You can easily avoid this problem by ensuring the quality of your koi's diet. Simply feeding it additional foods like spinach, turnip greens, broccoli florets, and dark green leafy lettuce will go a long way to keeping your koi's vitamin C levels up.

It's essential that your commercial koi food isn't older than 90 days. When you do buy your food, make sure it contains ascorbic acid.

Scoliosis can be held in check if detected early enough. As soon as you discover the problem, remove the affected fish to the quarantine tank. You can then concentrate on an individualized diet for the fish.

Scoliosis may develop in any of your rapidly growing fish. The extra vitamin C is an excellent approach to supporting their health.

There are several other factors which also may trigger scoliosis. The first is a tryptophan deficiency. Your fish may not be getting enough of this amino acid in their diet.

Essential for creating protein, tryptophan may be missing because it's being lost in the food even before it gets to your koi. To prevent this situation, try using -- if you can -- two different, high-quality staple diets.

Supplement your fish's diet with mealworms and crickets. You may want to partially crush these first. Earthworms or other bait worms also make good supplements.

Scoliosis may be caused by a trauma. The muscles of koi are wrapped around them in bands referred to as somites. When one of these somites is damaged, it may actually die. Then it naturally shrinks, which in turn, "kinks" the fish. It wil look especially "kinked" when it's swimming, even though the fish may look perfectly normal while resting.

And finally, your koi may develop scoliosis through the use of certain medications, most notably, organophosphates, trichlorfon, or malathion.

These drugs can actually cause body kinking through the hyper-contraction of the muscles.

You're not going to recognize the symptoms of all the disease right away, but knowing when something is amiss is the first step toward helping your fish. As soon as you think one koi may be developing a problem, don't hesitate to quarantine it.

After all, it's better to be wrong than to not act and lose your entire pond!

Speaking of ponds, the next chapter is devoted to those ambitious -- or enthusiastic -- individuals who want to learn more about constructing a koi pond on their own. Yes, more people than you can imagine actually plan, design, and build their own pond.

What I present in the following chapter is just a quick overview, but it will give you an idea of steps involved and help you decide whether you're up to the challenge.

Chapter 7:
Planning and Installing
Your Own Koi Pond

To build or not to build, that is the question. You're right; that's not exactly how Shakespeare phrased it. But Kevin Costner's dream in *Field of Dreams* gets us a little closer to the answer: Build it, and they will come.

Okay, so we have to modify that, too. Build it, then stock it with koi, and enjoy it!

If you're thinking about building your own pond for koi, you're in good company. Thousands of people are doing it all the time. I'm giving you fair warning, though -- it really is an ambitious undertaking and not for the faint of heart.

On the other hand, the rewards of building your own pond are amazing. Before you decide, why not read this chapter over? It gives you a good idea of what's involved. Then you can decide if you want to give it a try.

Construction
Considerations

Even before you design your pond, ponder

these points about its overall construction and appearance. A little planning before you jump in may help minimize your regrets later on.

First, don't skimp on size. Make it as big as your space and budget allow right from the start.

Most koi parents start their project believing a pond holding 500 to 2,000 gallons will be quite big enough. But as we develop into avid koi keepers and our appreciation of the fish increases (or as our spouses say, we become addicted), we realize the first pond isn't nearly big enough.

Our desire -- or need, if you will -- is to acquire even more koi. Sooner than we think, we're talking about building another pond -- perhaps one that can hold 10,000 even 50,000 gallons of water.

Just think about it for a moment. If you build a pond holding a mere 2,000 gallons, you can only put 20 full-size adult koi in it, at most.

Dig Deep!

Not only do you want it as large as possible, give serious thought to making your pond as deep as you possibly can. Four feet is not too deep. I don't choose that depth arbitrarily, either.

Four feet deep protects your pond from raccoons, if you have any in your area. Raccoons simply love the taste of koi.

Even eight feet isn't too deep. Yes, that means you wouldn't be able to stand up in your pond. And it also doubles the size of your structure. But it offers more protection -- this time from great blue herons and kingfishers.

Consider constructing your pond somewhere you can place a bird net over it. You know those blue herons I warned you about in the previous paragraph? They really are a threat to the stability of your pond.

A single heron can eat at least 100 six-inch koi in one meal. Now that's an appetite! If you live in Colorado, the herons can cost you money (and lots of it), particularly in the months of May and June. That's when they're feeding their young.

Build your pond in an area where it won't get direct sunlight the entire day. Five to six hours are about the maximum your koi can handle. As part of their protection from direct sunlight, you may want to plant water lilies or other items that will shade the water. We've talked briefly about this when we talked about the quarantine tank.

But, before you build your pond under a tree, think long and hard. You'll have leaves and needles to deal with in your koi pond on a regular basis.

Give some thought to the size of the water pump you'll need for the pond as well. The pump, filtration, and an ultraviolet sterilizer all need to be large enough. Check with your local equipment dealers and go over all your options.

Got Winter?
Think Ahead!

Does your area get a cold winter? Mine does. Consider buying and installing an inexpensive cattle trough heater. This will allow you to keep a hole in the ice when the weather turns cold. A trough heater can be purchased either in 1,000 or 1,500 watts.

Another way to keep your pond from completely freezing over is to keep the water moving. Aeration can help with this. However you approach this, the last thing you want is a solid ice cap over your entire pond.

If your budget will allow it, condiser installing a gas heater. One of the characteristics of koi is that when their water temperature gets colder than 50 degrees, they stop eating. And when they stop eating, they stop growing.

A gas pond heater lengthens their growing season, which in turn means they'll grow bigger faster. A gas heater also reduces the normal fluctuations inherent in a hot day and a cold night.

Reduce Organic
Materials

This next tip is aimed at the reduction of the organic material that causes the foam under your waterfall. You can reduce this material by installing a protein skimmer. You're right – very few pond owners use them. But it's a great idea, and you should try to budget for it.

As part of your maintenance program, consider replacing five to 10 percent of the water in your pond on a weekly basis. In this way, your water is kept fresh and the process helps to reduce the buildup of those organics.

If you decide to do this, you may have to replace your chemicals more often as well.

Once you've built and stocked your pond, remember that chlorinated water kills koi. Don't forget to buffer the pH levels in the water. You'll have to continuously monitor the ammonia and nitrite levels in your pond as well.

Not only can the presence of these elements kill your koi, but they can also reveal secrets about the status of your water quality. Keeping an eye on these levels can tell you if you're over feeding your fish, or if overcrowding is occurring.

Other chemicals and minerals you must test for regularly include chlorine, alkalinity, salinity, nitrate oxygen, copper, and phosphate.

When you're stocking your pond, don't place any goldfish in it. There is a practical reason for this: goldfish are a lot like rabbits. They breed very easily. Before you know it, you'll have more goldfish than you really want. Keep it to koi!

Where To Start?

Building the Pond

Starting at the beginning means you deciding where you want to put your pond.

I can't help you with an exact location; you know your yard best. Maybe you've already been dreaming about where you'd put your pond. If so, inspect this area again.

Stake the area off. You can use something as simple as a garden hose to outline the area you're considering digging. The hose is flexible enough to give you rounded edges, and sturdy enough to stay in place.

We've already mentioned the most important elements it should include: it should be shade-free for five to six hours of the day. You should have some water lilies or other shade for your koi, as well as adequate protection from strong winds.

One more consideration -- a purely practical one. Your pond needs to have convenient access to both water and electricity. You'll also want the pond as close to the house as you can make it, so you can enjoy it more fully. (Okay, so this last one -- enjoyment -- isn't as practical as the others!)

Removing the Earth

"Removing the earth" sounds nice, but in plain, everyday English, you're digging a hole. Now we're getting into the potentially back-breaking, labor-intensive part of pond building.

Face it, few of us are really up to digging an eight-foot deep pond. This can be solved easily by hiring an earth mover to complete the excavating.

Of course, you shouldn't dig before you consult with your utility companies. The staff at these businesses can determine whether there are any underground cables in your selected pond spot.

Maintaining a Shelf Area

When you dig, you'll want to include a "shelf" area around the inside of the dug-out pond. This is a great location to place marginal plants in containers. Then you can place any deep water aquatic plants on the bottom of the pond itself.

Once you have the hole dug, you'll place the pond liner across the dug-out pond. Weight this down with rocks for the moment.

Now fill the pond with water. Don't worry about the liner at this point. It'll stretch to match the contours of the hole. As the pond fills, you can then begin to remove a portion of the rocks. This allows the liner to gradually move into the dug out area.

Once you have the pond filled, except for the top two inches, turn off the water. Remove all the stones from the pond and then cut the edge around the liner. You can easily do this with a pair of scissors.

Why Use a Liner?

You may be wondering why I'm mentioning a liner. Well, for one thing, a flexible liner really makes it easier to build a natural-looking waterfall.

Yes, you can design a waterfall yourself. You probably have something in mind already. It's not difficult to make that vision a reality.

Take separate liner sheets for each tier you desire. Overlap them if necessary. Each of the levels should slope backwards to form a pool. Then you can use a projecting stone at the front to form a weir. Place the riverbed stones in mortar on the sides and bottom and you'll discover you have a quite attractive and natural-looking setting.

Next, lay your choice of rocks around the edge of the pond. You want them to lay over the edge toward the inside of the pond, about one to two inches. This helps to hide the edge of the liner.

After all the stones have been laid out, place mortar among them to hold the rocks together. As you do this, place some smaller rocks around the larger ones to fill in any gaps. This ensures the entire liner is completely covered.

Careful With That Mortar!

Placing mortar in between these rocks can be a painstaking job. It's far too easy to drop mortar into the water. Mortar has lime in it. If you should accidently drop any mortar into the pond itself, empty it immediately. That's irritating, to say the least -- and we're not talking about cost yet!

Once you have the water and the design just the way you want, you're not ready to start introducing your koi to their new home. Not until you've ensured the quality of the water. We've talked about this throughout the book, so you have a rough overview of this topic. But it really is important. One more paragraph discussing it -- and emphasizing it -- is in order.

I've talked about the need to keep the acid content -- also known as the pH balance -- of your pond low. The reason for this is simple, even though I haven't put it quite so bluntly before: high aciditic levels actually suffocate your fish.

So before you place your first koi in the pond, be sure to perform all the necessary testing.

It's essential that you install some form of filtration and aeration system. Many experts believe that your best choice would be a mechanical filter combined with biological and UV filters.

They also estimate that the biological filters need at least two to three months to mature. If you want to place koi in your pond before this, then you need to provide a chemical backup.

The great thing about having good filtration in your pond is that it improves overall aeration of the system as well. Another way to maintain good aeration is with that waterfall you've just constructed. Some koi parents create water fountains in the ponds for this reason.

Now wipe the sweat off that brow! Say, "Whew!" And begin to think about stocking your pond. Yep, you're actually that far along!

Placing the plants

You can start by placing the water plants into the pond. Simply set the pots onto the shelf and on the bottom of the pond itself. After this, wait a full week before introducing fish into your pond.

How many fish fill a pond? No, this isn't a joke. It's a serious question you should be asking yourself right about now. The rule of thumb is that for every "inch of fish" you need 25 square feet of pond space.

Now, you're ready! Finally! It's time to sit back, pour yourself that tall glass of ice tea, and enjoy your koi!

Congratulations.

Koi Clubs USA

8305 West Sample Rd. #4
Coral Springs, Florida 33065
954-753-9596
Fax : 954-753-9596
http://www.koiclubsusa.com/

Associated Koi Clubs of America

http://www.akca.org/joomla/index.php

Koi USA Magazine

http://www.koiusa.com/

When you pick up those keys and head out the door to buy your koi, you have a whole list of items to think about -- from the conditions of the breeder to the health of the individual fish.

This can put strain on even the most experienced of koi parents, but if you're new to this ritual, it can be downright nerve-racking. That's why I created **The Ultimate Koi Checklist**. Just print this out the next time you're koi shopping and take it with you. In other words, don't leave home without it!

Questions you must ask or factors you must notice include:

Are the display tanks clean?
Are the display tanks bio-filtered?
Does each tank have its own filter?
Does this establishment quarantine new fish? For how long?
Can you obtain background information on the koi of your choosing?

Discovering this information is important. Koi with good backgrounds cost more --

sometimes lots more -- than your average koi. You may find a dealer who swears up and down that he's selling you "Japanese koi." He may tell you that's why your pick is so expensive. But unless you see the background information on that fish to confirm it, don't believe it.

Of course, if it really is a special fish and you have the money, then by all means consider purchasing it. These fish, to be quite blunt about it, are of a higher quality.

Ai: The Japanese preface used in the description of koi meaning blue or indigo.

Aigoromo: A specific variety of koi -- the goromo -- with blue or indigo appearance.

Ai Showa: A specific variety of koi -- the Showa - with blue or indigo markings.

Aka: The Japanese preface used in the description of koi meaning red.

Akame: The eye of a koi having a red iris.

Akebi: The Japanese preface used in the description of the colorings of koi meaning light blue.

Asagi: This term for blue refers to koi with a specific appearance of a bluish body and red markings on the underside, which may also appear on the pectoral fins and cheeks.

Ato sumi: This describes black markings which developed late on a fish.

Bekko: This description is given to a fish with a single base color -- such as white, red, or yellow -- which also has black markings. Generally, these markings take the form of spots or speckles above the lateral line.

Beni: The Japanese preface describing a koi with orange-red markings.

Boke: Koi term referring to a faded or blurred color, and usually referring specifically to a faded or blurred black (or sumi).

Budo: A color that is between aigoromo and sumigoromo.

Bunka: A variation of the sanshoku or the three color pattern.

Cha: The Japanese preface used to describe the brown in a koi fish.

Chagoi: A brown koi, which is noted for its splendid growth.

Doitsu: Derived from the Japanese for "German," this refers to a koi with no visible scales, or one who has mirror-like scales on the dorsal and lateral lines.

Enyu: This is a doitsu koi with a white body, red markings, and platinum mirror scales. Additionally, this variety has pale blue speckles which maybe interspersed within the red and white color of his dorsal surface.

Etsu No Hisoku: A doitsu koi that's yellow-green.

Fukurin: The area around the scales of a metallic koi that displays more luster than the other areas.

Gin: Refers to the silver metallic color of a koi.

Ginrin: A koi with silver-colored sparkling scales. (Sometimes you'll see this as two words.)

Goior Koi or **Goi:** Wild carp.

Goke: A fish scale.

Gosanke: A term which refers to the three major varieties of koi: Kohaku, Sanke, and Showa.

Goshiki: Literally translates from Japanese into "five colors." Refers to a koi with a white base color, a black and blue appearance, overlaid with red patterns similar to the Kahaku.

Gotensakura: A Kohaku variety of koi with an abundance of red spots.

Hageshiro: An all-black koi except for his head and snout, which are patched with white or brown.

Hagoroma: A specific variety of the aigoromo.

Hajiro: An all-black koi except for its tail and fins, which are edged in white.

Hanako: The term refers to a red koi. Literally the word translates to "flower maiden."

Hi: The Japanese koi term for red, usually used to describe a red patch or coloration on a koi.

Hariwake: Term used to describe a white, metallic koi with gold or yellow markings.

Hikari: The term for "metallic."

Hikarimoyo: This term refers to a metallic koi with more than one color. The exceptions are the metallic showa and the metallic utsuri. Both of these are classified as Hikari utsuri.

Hikarimuju: This term refers to metallic variety of either the showa or the utsuri.

Hisoku: The koi term for the yellow-green color found on these fish.

Inazuma: The zigzag pattern most associated with the Kohaku variety of koi.

Jiro: The word used to describe white when talking about koi.

Kabuto: This term refers to a koi whose head is a different color than its body. Literally, the word means "helmet."

Kagami: An older variety of koi possessing mirror scales on the dorsal and ventral sides.

Kanako: A koi possessing a white body with red spots.

Karasu: A pure black koi, very often tinged with a bluish haze.

Kasane Sumi: The term refers to a black marking on a red background.

Kawa: A koi with only a few scales on the area of its dorsal surface, and these scales are reflective. Otherwise it has no scales.

Kawarimono: An older, more traditional name for the koi with an undefined color or pattern.

Kawarigo: The newer, modern term which refers to Kawarimono Koi. This term covers all koi varieties that don't fall under any other established recognized classifications.

Ki: The Japanese koi term for yellow.

Kin: The Japanese koi term for metallic gold.

Kiwa: The term referring to the edge of a patch or marking.

Kinginrin: The term which refers to a koi with silver- or gold-colored sparkling scales.

Kinrin: The term used when talking about a koi with gold-colored sparkling scales.

Kohaku: Koi with a white body and red markings.

Komoyo: The small zigzag pattern of red and white found on koi.

Konjo: The koi term that refers to dark blue.

Koromo: Literally, this word translates to "robed." It refers to a koi that has a base color of white with red patterns overlaid with dark appearance.

Koshi: The koi word that refers to green.

Kuchibeni: A koi with red lips.

Kujaku: This term refers to a metallic koi with red, orange, or golden markings. Literally translates to "peacock."

Kumonryu: Term used to describe a doitsu koi with what many call a "killer whale" pattern: a black body with white markings.

Kuro: The term used for black.

Leather Koi: The phrase used for a koi that has no visible scales.

Ma: The term used for "wild."

Maruten: Refers to a koi whose head possesses a round red patch, as well as other markings on its body.

137

Matsuba: A pattern which resembles a pine cone, usually caused by scales with different colors in the centers than on the edges.

Menkaburi: The term for a Kahaku koi with a total head of red. Literally means "masked."

Menware: Refers to the lightning-shaped marking on the head of a koi. This pattern is actually desirable in the showa and the utsuri.

Meija: The era that began in 1868 and ended in 1912.

Midorigoi: Refers to a doitsu koi that has a greenish color.

Motoaka: Term used to describe a red pectoral joint.

Motoguro: Term which describes the black at the base of the pectoral fins, a desirable trait in the utsuri and the showa.

Moyo: Term which refers to markings or patterns in general.

Muji: Literally translates to "nothing else." Usually used as a suffix to describe a koi with only one color.

Narumi: Term meaning light blue.

Nezu: Term for a gray or tarnished silver color on koi.

Ni: The Japanese word for "two."

Nidan: This term refers to a two-stepped Kohaku, a koi with two red patches over a white body.

Odome: This word refers to a tail stop.

Ogon: A word used to describe a single-colored metallic koi.

Omoyo: A single-stepped Kohaku. This koi has one patch over its white body.

Orenji: The Japanese term for orange.

Purachina: The term used to describe a platinum or white metallic koi.

Rin: The term koi keepers use to refer to a scale.

Sandan: A three-stepped Kohaku -- a koi possessing three red patches on a white body.

Sashi: This word describes a koi with mottled black, gray, or blue colors beneath its skin. Most often the term refers to black markings which are not fully developed. It may also be used to refer to a blurred line that caused by white scales which overlap red ones of the hi.

Shiro: Japanese word meaning white.

Shiroji: White background.

Shiku: Colored.

Shimi: Refers to undesirable small black spots dotting the body of koi.

Showa: A koi possessing a black body with red and white markings.   The black markings are typically in the form of large streaks wrapped around the body.

Shusui: A doitsu koi with dorsal coloring of light blue, ventral colorations of red, and mirror scales.

Sui: A term which describes a ripple effect.

Sumi: A black marking or patch.

Taisho Era: The era in Japanese history

starting with 1912 and ending in 1926.

Taish Sanshoku: Another name for the sanke koi.

Tancho: Any kohaku, sanke, or showa koi with only a single red marking that is round and located on the head of the fish.

Taegu: Any koi with the potential to be a future champion in a koi show.

Toby Hi: A term used to describe a pattern that resembled red merely "splattered" on the fish.

Today: Any koi younger than one year.

Stub Sumi: The term referring to a pattern of black markings over a white background.

Usturi: A koi whose body is one color -- white, red, or yellow -- and possesses black markings. The markings typically resemble streaks wrapping around the body.

Yamabuki: The term refers to a pale yellow. It gets this description from the name of a yellow-petaled rose from China.

Yamabuki ogon: A single-colored metallic

141

koi that is pale yellow.

Yamabuki Hariwake: A metallic koi possessing a white body and light yellow markings.

Yondan: A four-stepped kohaku -- a fish with four red patches on its white body.

Yotsujiro: A black koi with white head, fins, and undersides.

Yoroi: Literally translate into "armored" and refers to the doitus koi who possess an excessive amount of mirror scales.

Zuiun: This term refers to a color variant of the shusui.

References

Web Sites

Koi, http://en.wikipedia.org/wiki/Koi, accessed 6 Apr 10.

Koi Varieties, http://www.wetwebmedia.com/pondsubweb index/koivarieties.htm, accessed 7 April 10.

Koi Selection, http://www.wetwebmedia.com/PondSubWe bIndex/koiselart.htm, 7 Apr 10.

How To Determine Sex: Koi, http://www.pond-doctor.co.uk/longsexkoi.html, accessed 8 Apr 10.

Koi Care: Quarantine Your New Koi, http://www.nishikigoi-info.com/koi-care/quarantine.html, accessed 9 Apr 10.

Koi Care: Why Quarantine? http://www.bonniesplants.com/sick_injured _fish/quarantine.htm accessed 10 Apr 10.

Like Oil and Water, Koi Ponds and Algae Don't Mix, http://www.naturalenviro.com/Article.php?

ArticleSKU=Koi-Pond-Algae, accessed 14 Apr 10.

Algae Control, http://www.lagunakoi.com/Algae-Control-Library-sc-336.html, accessed 14 Apr 10.

http://www.fishyfarmacy.com/koi_pond.html, accessed 14 Apr 10.

Stress Removal is Essential to Maintain Disease Free Healthy Koi, http://www.garden-pond-filters.com/koihealthycondition.htm, accessed 15 Apr 10.

Relevant Koi Diseases, http://www.akca.org/library/diease4.htm, accessed 15 Apr 10.

Building a Koi Pond, http://www.koifishponds.com/building.htm, accessed 16 Apr 10.

How to Build a Koi Pond, http://www.abcponds.com/koi-ponds/building-koi-ponds.htm, accessed 17 Apr 10

Books

Bartlett, R.D., and Bartlett, Patricia, **Koi for**

Dummies, Wiley Publishing, Hoboken, NJ, 2007.

Blasiola, George C., ***Koi, Barron's Complete Pet Owner's Manuals,*** Barron's Educational Series, 1995.

DeVito, Carlo, and Skomal, Gregory, ***The Everything Tropical Fish Book,*** Everything Books, 2000.

Printed in Great Britain
by Amazon.co.uk, Ltd.,
Marston Gate.